Spanish Rhymes

Illustrated by Lynda Taylor

HOUGHTON MIFFLIN COMPANY

BOSTON

ATLANTA   DALLAS   GENEVA, ILLINOIS   PALO ALTO   PRINCETON

RIMA DE CHOCOLATE

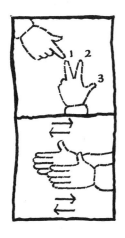

Uno, dos, tres, cho-

Uno, dos, tres, -co-

Uno, dos, tres, -la-

Uno, dos, tres, -te

Bate, bate chocolate.

CHOCOLATE RHYME

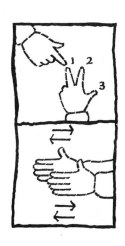

One, two, three, cho-

One, two, three, -co-

One, two, three, -la-

One, two, three, -te

Stir, stir the chocolate.

LOS PESCADITOS

Los pescaditos andan en el agua,

nadan, nadan, nadan.

Vuelan, vuelan, vuelan.

Son chiquititos, chiquititos.

Vuelan, vuelan, vuelan.

Nadan, nadan, nadan.

4

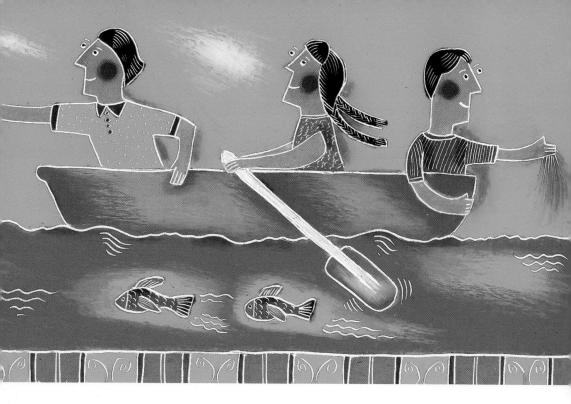

LITTLE FISH

Little fish move in the water,

swim, swim, swim.

Fly, fly, fly.

Little ones, little ones.

Fly, fly, fly.

Swim, swim, swim.

LOS POLLITOS

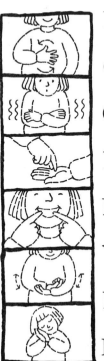

Los pollitos dicen: —pío, pío, pío,

Cuando tienen hambre,

Cuando tienen frío.

La gallina busca el maíz y el trigo.

Les da la comida,

Y les presta abrigo.

Bajo sus dos alas, acurrucaditos,

Hasta el otro día duermen los pollitos

6

THE CHICKS

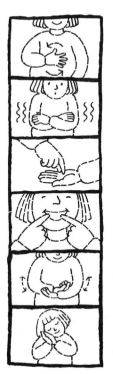

The little chicks say, "Peep, peep, peep,"

When they are hungry,

When they are cold.

The hen looks for corn and wheat.

She gives them food,

And she keeps them warm.

Huddling under her wings,

They sleep until the next day.